Ho[illegible]y

BROCKHAMPTON PRESS
LONDON

This edition published 1996 by Brockhampton Press,
a member of Hodder Headline PLC Group.

ISBN 1 86019 267 X

Printed and bound in the UK

Introduction

The aim of homoeopathy is to cure an illness or disorder by treating the whole person, rather than merely concentrating on a set of symptoms. Hence, in homoeopathy the approach is holistic and the overall state of health of the patient, especially his or her emotional and psychological wellbeing, are regarded as being very significant. A homoeopath notes the symptoms that the person wishes to have cured, but also takes time to discover other signs or indications of disorder which the patient may regard as being less important. The reasoning behind this is that illness is a sign of disorder or imbalance within the body. It is believed that the whole 'make up' of a person determines, to a great extent, the type of disorders to which that individual is prone, and the symptoms likely to occur. A homoeopathic remedy must be suitable both for the symptoms and the characteristics and temperament of the patient. Hence two patients with the same illness may be offered different remedies according to their individual nature. One remedy may also be used to treat different groups of symptoms or ailments.

Homoeopathic remedies are based on the concept that 'like cures like', an ancient philosophy which can be traced back to the fifth century BC, when it was formulated by Hippocrates. In the early 1800s, this idea awakened the interest of a German doctor, Samuel Hahnemann, who believed that the medical practices at that time were too harsh and tended to hinder rather than aid healing. Hahnemann observed that a treatment for malaria, based on an extract of cinchona bark (quinine), actually produced symptoms of this disease when taken in a small dose by a healthy person. Further extensive studies convinced him that the production of symptoms was the body's way of combating illness. Hence, a minute dose of a substance which stimulated the symptoms of an illness in a healthy person, could be used to fight that illness in someone who was sick. Hahnemann conducted numerous trials (called 'provings') giving minute doses of substances to healthy people and recording the symptoms produced. Eventually, these very dilute remedies were given to people with illnesses, often with very encouraging results.

Modern homoeopathy is based on the work of Hahnemann, and the medicines derived from plant, mineral and animal sources are used in extremely dilute amounts. Indeed it is believed that the curative properties are enhanced by each dilution because impurities which might cause unwanted side effects are lost. Substances used in homoeopathy are first soaked in alcohol to extract their essential ingredients. This initial solution, called the 'mother tincture' is diluted successively either by factors of ten (called the 'decimal scale' and designated X), or 100 (the 'centesimal scale' and designated C). Each dilution is shaken vigorously before further ones are made and this is thought to make the properties more powerful by adding energy at each stage, while impurities are removed. The thorough shaking of each dilution is said to energize or 'potentiate' the medicine. The remedies are made into tablets or may be used in the form of ointment, solutions, powders, suppositories etc. High potency (i.e. more dilute) remedies are used for severe symptoms and lower potency (less dilute) for milder ones.

The homoeopathic view is that during the process of healing, symptoms are redirected from more important to less important body systems. It is also held that healing is from innermost to outermost parts of the body and that more recent symptoms disappear first, this being known as the 'law of direction of cure'. Occasionally, symptoms may worsen initially when a homoeopathic remedy is taken, but this is usually short-lived and is known as a 'healing crisis.' It is taken to indicate a change and that improvement is likely to follow. Usually, with a homoeopathic remedy, an improvement is noticed fairly quickly although this depends upon the nature of the ailment, health, age and wellbeing of the patient and the potency of the remedy.

A first homoeopathic consultation is likely to last about one hour so that the specialist can obtain a full picture of the patient's medical history and personal circumstances. On the basis of this information, the homoeopathic practitioner decides on an appropriate remedy and potency. Subsequent consultations are generally shorter and full advice is given on how to store and take the medicine. It is widely accepted that homoeopathic remedies are very safe and non-addictive but they are covered by the legal requirements governing all medicines and should be obtained from a recognized source.

Potency table for homoeopathic medicines

The centesimal scale

1C = 1/100 (1/1001) of 'mother tincture'
2C = 1/10 000 (1/1002) of 'mother tincture'
3C = 1/1 000 000 (1/1003) of 'mother tincture'
6C = 1/1 000 000 000 000 (1/1006) of 'mother tincture'

The decimal scale

1X = 1/10 (1/101) of 'mother tincture'
2X = 1/100 (1/102) of 'mother tincture'
6X = 1/000 000 (1/106) of 'mother tincture'

Homoeopathic remedies in common use

Aconitum nepellus

Aconite, Monkshood, Wolfbane, Friar's Cap, Mousebane

Aconitum is a native plant of Switzerland and other mountainous regions of Europe where it grows in the damp conditions of alpine meadows. Attractive purple/ dark blue flowers are borne on tall, upright stems produced from tubers developed from the root system. Aconite is highly poisonous and its sap was used by ancient hunters on the end of their arrows. 'Wolfsbane' refers to this use, and aconitum is derived from the Latin word *acon* meaning dart. This was one of the homoeopathic remedies extensively tested and proved by Hahnemann. He used it for the acute infections and fevers, accompanied by severe pain, which were usually treated by blood-letting by the physicians of his day. This remains its main use in modern homoeopathy and the whole plant is used to produce the remedy.

Aconite is a valuable treatment for acute illnesses of rapid onset in people who have previously been healthy and well. These often occur after the person has been out in cold wet weather. It is used especially at the start of feverish respiratory infections such as colds and influenza and those affecting the eyes and ears. The person usually experiences restlessness, a hot, flushed face and pains and disturbed sleep but may be pale when first getting up. It is also used to treat the menopausal symptoms of hot flushes. It is an effective remedy for some mental symptoms including extreme anxiety and fear, palpitations and attacks of panic, especially the belief that death is imminent during illness. The remedy encourages sweating and is sometimes used in conjunction with belladonna. Symptoms are made worse by cold, draughts, tobacco smoke, stuffy, airless, warm rooms, listening to music, at midnight and by lying on the painful part. They improve out in the fresh air and with warmth. The person who benefits from aconite is typically strong, solid or well-built, high-coloured and usually enjoys good health but has a poor opinion of himself. Due to this he (or she) tends to have a constant need to prove his own worth, to the point of insensitivity or unkindness to others. When in good health, aconite people have a need for the company of others. However, they also have fears which they keep concealed and may be frightened of going out or being in a crowd. When ill, they are inclined to be morbid, believing that death is imminent, and they cope badly with any kind of shock.

Actea racemosa

Cimic., Cimifuga racemosa, Black Snakeroot, Rattleroot, Bugbane, Rattleweed, Squaw Root.

This plant is a native of woodlands in Canada and the United States and was used by American Indians as a remedy for the bite of the rattlesnake. It was also used as a tranquillizer and for pain relief in labour and menstruation. An infusion made from the plant was sprinkled in the home to protect against supernatural forces and evil spirits. The plant has a dark, woody underground stem (rhizome) and roots and produces feathery, tall stems of white flowers. The fresh rhizomes and roots are used in homoeopathy, being collected, cut and dried in the autumn, after the stems and leaves have died down and the fruit has been formed. The rhizome has a faint, unpleasant smell and the taste is acrid and bitter. The remedy was extensively tested and proved by an English homoeopath, Dr Richard Hughes, who used it in the treatment of a stiff neck and associated headache. It is used for this purpose in modern homoeopathy and also to treat pain in the lower back and between the shoulder blades. Also, for rheumatic pain and swelling of joints or muscles and other sudden, sharp pains. Actaea is considered to be of great value in the treatment of menstrual problems with cramps, bloatedness and pain and symptoms of pregnancy, e.g. morning sickness and abdominal discomfort. It is also of value for postnatal depression and menopausal symptoms. Emotional symptoms which accompany these periods of hormonal change, such as weepiness, anxiety and irritability are also eased by this remedy. Symptoms are made worse by exposure to cold, wet, draughty conditions, by any sudden change in the weather, on drinking alcohol and with excitement. They improve with keeping warm, with gentle exercise and in the fresh, open air. A person suitable for this remedy is often a woman who may be bubbly, extrovert and talkative or withdrawn, depressed and sad, heaving great sighs. She is usually emotionally intense with a fear of dying and madness. These fears are at their height in a woman going through the menopause.

Allium

Allium cepa; Spanish onion

The onion has been cultivated and used for many centuries, both for culinary and medicinal purposes and was important in ancient Egyptian civilization. The volatile oil released when an onion is sliced stimulates the tear glands of the eyes and mucous membranes of the nose, throat and air passages. Hence, in homoeopathy, the onion is used to treat ailments with symptoms of a streaming nose and watering eyes. The red Spanish onion, cultivated throughout the world, is used to make the homoeopathic remedy. It is used to treat allergic conditions such as hay fever, colds and pains or symptoms which go from one side to the other. It is useful for shooting, stabbing or burning pains associated with neuralgia, which may alternate from side to side, frontal headaches, painful molar teeth and earache in children. The symptoms worsen in cold, damp conditions and improve in fresh air and cool, dry surroundings.

Apis mellifica

Apis; Apis mellifera, the honey bee

The source of the medicine is the entire body of the honey bee which is crushed or ground to prepare the remedy. It is used particularly to treat inflammation, redness, swelling and itching of the skin which is sensitive to touch, and with stinging hot pains. There is usually feverishness and thirst and the pains are worsened by heat and relieved by cold. The remedy is used for insect stings, nettle rash, allergic conditions, blisters, whitlow (an abscess on the finger tip) and infections of the urinary tract, including cystitis, with stabbing hot pains. Also for urinary incontinence in elderly persons, fluid retention causing swelling of the eyelids or other areas, allergic conditions which cause sore throat and swallowing difficulty and tonsillitis. The person often experiences hot, stabbing headaches and has dry skin. Apis is additionally valued as a remedy for swollen, painful inflammation of the joints, as in arthritic conditions, and for peritonitis and pleurisy. Symptoms are made worse by heat and touch, stuffy airless rooms, after sleep and in the early evening. They improve in the fresh, cool open air, after taking a cold bath or any cold application. A person suitable for the apis remedy tends to expect high standards and may be rather irritable and hard to please. He (or she) likes to organize others and is protective of his own domain, tending to be resentful of anyone new. Apis types may seem to be rushing around and working hard but may achieve very little as a result.

Argenticum nitricum

Argent nit; silver nitrate, Devil's Stone, lunar caustic, Hellstone

Silver nitrate is obtained from the mineral acanthite, which is a natural ore of silver. White silver nitrate crystals are derived from a chemical solution of the mineral ore and these are used to make the homoeopathic remedy. Silver nitrate is poisonous in large doses and has antiseptic and caustic properties. In the past it was used to clean out wounds and prevent infection. In homoeopathy, it is used to treat states of great anxiety, panic, fear or apprehension about a forthcoming event, e.g. taking an examination, having to perform a public role (speech-making, chairing a public meeting, acting, singing), going for an interview or any activity involving scrutiny and criticism by others. It was also used as a remedy for digestive complaints including indigestion, abdominal pain, wind, nausea and headache. Often, there is a longing for sweet 'comfort' or other types of food. This remedy may be given for laryngitis, sore throat and hoarseness, eye inflammation such as conjunctivitis and period pains. Other types of pain, asthma, and warts may also benefit.

Often, a person experiences symptoms mainly on the left side and these are worse for heat and at night. Also, they are made worse by anxiety and overwork, emotional tension and resting on the left side. Pains are made worse with talking and movement. Symptoms improve in cold or cool fresh air and are relieved by belching. Pains are helped by applying pressure to the painful part. People suitable for argent are quick-witted and rapid in thought and action. They may appear outgoing and happy but are a prey to worry, anxiety and ungrounded fears which make them tense. All the emotions are quick to surface and tey are able to put on an impressive performance. They enjoy a wide variety of foods, particularly salty and sweet things although these may upset the digestion. They have a fear of heights, crowds, of being burgled, of failure and arriving late for an appointment. Also, of serious illness, dying and madness. argent people are generally slim and full of restless energy and tension. They may have deeply etched features and lines on the skin which make them appear older than their real age.

Arnica montana

Arnica; Leopard's Bane, Sneezewort, Mountain tobacco

Arnica is a native plant of woodland and mountainous regions of central Europe and Siberia. It has a dark-brown root system from which a central stem arises, producing pairs of elongated green leaves and bright yellow flowers. If the flowers are crushed or bruised and a person then inhales the scent, this causes sneezing. All the fresh parts of the flowering plant are used to prepare the homoeopathic remedy. It is a commonly used first aid remedy for symptoms relating to injury or trauma of any kind, e.g. bruising, swelling, pain and bleeding. It is also used to treat physical and mental shock. It is helpful following surgery, childbirth or tooth extraction, promoting healing, and also for gout, rheumatic joints with pain, heat and inflammation, sore sprained or strained muscles, concussion, and osteoarthritis. Taken internally, it is a remedy for black eyes, eye strain and skin conditions such as eczema and boils. Arnica is helpful in the treatment of whooping cough in children and also wetting the bed when the cause is nightmares. Symptoms worsen with heat, touch and continued movement, and also with heat and resting for a long period. The symptoms improve when the person first begins to move and with lying down with the head at a lower level than the feet. A person suitable for treatment with this remedy tends to be solemn, fatalistic and subject to morbid fears. Arnica types usually deny the existence of any illness, even when obviously not well, and do not seek medical help, preferring to manage on their own.

Arsenicum album

Arsen alb; White arsenic trioxide

This is a widely used homoeopathic remedy, the source being white arsenic trioxide derived from arsenopyrite, a metallic mineral ore of arsenic. Arsenic has been known for centuries as a poison and was once used as a treatment for syphilis. White arsenic trioxide used to be given to improve muscles and skin in animals such as horses. It is used to treat acute conditions of the digestive system and chest and mental symptoms of anxiety and fear. Hence it is a remedy for diarrhoea and vomiting caused by eating the wrong kinds of food, or food poisoning or overindulgence in alcohol. Also, for dehydration in children following gastroenteritis or feverish illness. It is a remedy for asthma and breathing difficulties, mouth ulcers, a carbuncle (a collection of boils), dry, cracked lips, burning skin, inflamed, watering stinging eyes and psoriasis. Also, for sciatica, shingles, sore throat and painful swallowing, Candidiasis (fungal infection) of the mouth and motion sickness. There may be oedema (retention of fluid) showing as a puffiness around the ankles.

An ill person who benefits from this remedy experiences burning pains but also feels cold. The skin may be either hot or cold to the touch. The symptoms are worse for cold in any form, including cold food and drink, and between midnight and 3 a.m. They are worse on the right side and if the person is near the coast. Symptoms improve with warmth including warm drinks, gentle movement and lying down with the head raised. People suitable for treatment with this preparartion are precise, meticulous and ambitious and loathe any form of disorder. They are always immaculately dressed and everything in their life is neat and tidy. However, they tend to have great worries, especially about their financial security and their own health and that of their family. They fear illness and dying, loss of financial and personal status, being burgled, darkness and the supernatural. Arsenicum album people have strongly held views and do not readily tolerate contrary opinions or those with a more relaxed or disordered lifestyle. They enjoy a variety of different foods, coffee and alcoholic drinks. Physically, they are usually thin, with delicate, fine features and pale skin which may show worry lines. Their movements tend to be rapid and their manner serious and somewhat restless, although always polite.

Aurum metallicum

Aurum met.; Gold

Gold was highly prized by medieval Arabian physicians who used it to treat a variety of heart disorders. In the early part of this century, it was used in the treatment of tuberculosis. Gold is now used in conventional medicine for some cancer treatments and for rheumatic and arthritic complaints. In homoeopathy, pure gold is ground down to produce a fine powder and it is used to treat both physical and mental symptoms. It is used as a remedy for congestive circulatory disorders and heart diseases, including angina pectoris. The symptoms of this condition include a throbbing, pulsing headache, chest pain, breathlessness and palpitations. It is also used to treat liver disorders with symptoms of jaundice, painful conditions of bones and joints (especially the hip and knee joints), inflammation of the testes and an undescended testicle in small boys (especially if the right-side is affected). It is also a remedy for sinusitis and severe mental symptoms of despair, depression and thoughts of suicide. The person who is suitable for this remedy tends to drive himself very hard, to the point of being a workaholic. He (or she) is excessively conscientious but usually feels that he has not done enough and is oversensitive to the criticism of other people. The person may come to regard himself as a failure and become severely clinically depressed or even suicidal as a result. Symptoms are made worse by mental effort and concentration or physical exercise, especially in the evening or at night, and by emotional upheaval. They improve with cold bathing, walking in the fresh air and with rest and quiet.

Belladonna

Bell, Deadly Nightshade, Black Cherry, Devil's Cherries, Naughty Man's Cherries, Devil's Herb
Belladonna is a native plant of most of Europe although it is uncommon in Scotland. The plant is extremely

poisonous and many children have died as a result of being tempted to eat the shiny, black berries of Deadly Nightshade. It is a stout, stocky plant with light brown roots, growing to about four feet (1.2 metres) high, with green oval leaves and pale purple, bell-shaped flowers. In medieval times, the plant had its place in the potions of witchcraft. Italian women used extracts of the plant as eyedrops to widen the pupils of the eye and make them more beautiful. (Hence *bella donna* which means beautiful woman). The plant contains atropine, an alkaloid substance which induces paralysis of nerves and is used in orthodox medicine to relieve painful spasms and in ophthalmic (eye) procedures.

In homoeopathy, the remedy is obtained from the pulped leaves and flowers. It was investigated and proved by Hahnemann as a treatment for scarlet fever. Belladonna is used to treat acute conditions which arise suddenly, and in which there is a throbbing, pulsing headache and red, flushed skin, high fever and staring, wide eyes. The skin around the mouth and lips may be pale but the tongue is a fiery red and the hands and feet are cold. It is used as a remedy for infectious diseases such as influenza, scarlet fever, measles, whooping cough, chicken pox, mumps and the early stages of pneumonia. Also for boils, earache (particularly on the right side and worsened when the head is cold or wet), cystitis, boils, conjunctivitis, tonsillitis, inflammation of the kidneys, neuralgia (sharp pain along the course of a nerve) and sore throat. Other conditions which benefit from this remedy include labour pains, soreness of the breasts in breast-feeding, fever and teething in children, with broken sleep and whitlow (an infection of a finger nail). The symptoms are worse at night and with lying down, and occur more intensely on the right side. Also, they are exacerbated by loud noises, bright lights, jarring of the body, touch or pressure and with cool surroundings.

They improve with sitting upright or standing and keeping warm or with warm applications to the painful area. Belladonna people usually enjoy good health, being fit, energetic and ready to tackle any task. They are amusing, sociable and popular when in good health. However, if they become ill the reverse is often true and they may be restless, irritable and possibly even violent.

Bryonia alba

Bryonia, European White Bryony, Black-berried White Bryony, Wild Hops

Bryony is a native plant of many parts of Europe and grows in England, although it is rarely found in Scotland. It has large, white, branched roots with swollen, expanded portions which are highly poisonous. The smell given off is unpleasant and, if eaten, the taste is very bitter and death soon follows. The tall stems of the plant climb up supports by means of corkscrew tendrils and round, black berries are produced in the autumn. Bryony was used by the physicians of ancient Greece and Rome and was described by Hippocrates. The homoeopathic remedy is made from the fresh pulped root of the plant, and is mainly used for conditions producing acute stitch-like pains which are made worse by even slight movement, and relieved by rest. These ailments usually develop slowly and accompanying symptoms include dry skin, mouth and eyes with great thirst. It is used as a remedy for inflammation of the lining of joints in arthritic and rheumatic disorders with swelling, heat and pains. Also, for chest inflammation, pleurisy, chesty bronchitis and pneumonia with severe pain and dry, hacking cough. Digestive problems that are eased by bryonia include indigestion, colic, constipation, nausea, vomiting and diarrhoea. Breast inflammation due to breast-feeding, colic in babies, gout and lumbago may be helped by bryonia. The symptoms are made worse by movement and bending and improve with rest and pressure applied to the painful area. People suitable for bryonia are hard-working, conscientious and reliable but have a dread of poverty. They tend to measure success in life in financial or materialistic terms. They cope badly with any threat to their security or lifestyle, becoming extremely worried, fretful and depressed.

Calcarea Carbonica

Calc. carb; Calcium Carbonate

This important homoeopathic remedy is made from powdered mother-of-pearl, the beautiful, translucent inner layer of oyster shells. Calcium is an essential mineral in the body, being especially important for the healthy development of bones and teeth. This remedy is used to treat a number of different disorders especially those relating to bones and teeth, but also certain skin conditions and symptoms relating to the female reproductive system. It is a remedy for weak or slow growth of bones and teeth and fractures which take a long time to heal. Also, for teething problems in children, pains in bones, teeth and joints, headaches and eye inflammations affecting the right side, and ear infections with an unpleasant-smelling discharge. Premenstrual syndrome, heavy periods and menopausal disorders are helped by this remedy, as are chapped skin, eczema, verrucas and thrush infections.

People who benefit from treatment with this preparation are very sensitive to the cold, particularly in the hands and feet and tend to sweat profusely. They suffer from fatigue and anxiety, and body secretions (sweat and urine) smell unpleasant. Children who benefit have recurrent ear, nose and throat infections, especially tonsillitis and glue ear. Symptoms are made worse by draughts and cold, damp weather and also at night. They are worse when the person first wakens up in the morning and for physical exercise and sweating. In women, symptoms are worse premenstrually. They improve in warm, dry weather and are better later on in the morning and after the person has eaten breakfast. People suitable for this remedy are often overweight or even obese with a pale complexion. They are shy and very sensitive, quiet in company and always worried about what other people think of them. They are also hard-working, conscientious and reliable and easily upset by the suffering of others. They need constant reassurance from friends and family and tend to feel that they are a failure. Usually, they enjoy good health but have a tendency for skeletal weakness. They enjoy a wide variety of different foods and tend to overeat, but are upset by coffee and milk. They are afraid of dying and serious illness, the supernatural, madness, being a failure and becoming poor and they tend to be claustrophobic.

Calcarea fluorica

Calc fluor; fluorite, calcium fluoride, fluoride of lime
This homoeopathic remedy is one of the Schussler tissue salts. Calcium fluoride occurs naturally in the body in the enamel of the teeth, bones, skin and connective tissue. It is used to treat disorders of these body tissues or to maintain their elasticity. It is used to treat chronic lumbago, scars and to prevent the formation of adhesions

after operations, gout and arthritic nodules. Also, for rickets, slow growth of bones in children, enlarged adenoids which become stony due to persistent, recurrent respiratory tract infections and cataracts. It is used to strengthen weak tooth enamel and strained and stretched ligaments and muscles, e.g. around a joint. People suitable for this remedy are intelligent and punctual but tend to make mistakes through lack of planning. They benefit from the guidance of others to work efficiently and fear poverty and illness. They are often prone to piles, varicose veins, swollen glands and muscle and ligament strain. The manner of walking may be rapid with jerking of the limbs. Symptoms are made worse on beginning movement and in cold, damp, draughty conditions. They improve with warmth and heat and for continual gentle movement.

Calcarea phosphorica

Calc phos., phosphate of lime, calcium phosphate.
This homoeopathic remedy is a Schussler tissue salt and calcium phosphate is the mineral which gives hardness to bones and teeth. It is obtained by a chemical reaction between dilute phosphoric acid and calcium hydroxide, when a white precipitate of calcium phosphate is formed. Since calcium phosphate is an essential mineral in the normal, healthy development of bones and teeth, it is used to treat disorders in these tissues. It is particularly helpful as a remedy for painful bones, difficult fractures which are slow to heal, teeth prone to decay, problems of bone growth and teething in children and 'growing pains'. Also, it is beneficial during convalescence when a person is weakened and tired after an illness, and for digestive problems including diarrhoea, stomach pains and indigestion. It may be used as a remedy for

tonsillitis, sore throats and swollen glands. Children who benefit from this remedy tend to be thin, pale, miserable and fail to thrive, and are prone to sickness and headaches. They are often fretful and demanding. Adults are also unhappy and discontented with their circumstances, although they endeavour to be friendly towards others. They are restless and need plenty of different activities and stimulation, hating routine and needing a good reason to get out of bed in the morning. Symptoms are made worse by any change in the weather, and in cold, wet conditions, e.g. thawing snow. Also for worry or grief and too much physical activity. Symptoms improve when the weather is warm and dry, in summer, and from taking a hot bath.

Calendula officinalis

Calendula, Marigold, Garden Marigold, Marygold
This is a familiar garden plant which grows well in all parts of the United Kingdom, having light green leaves and bright orange flowers. The plant has been known for centuries for its healing properties and was used in the treatment of various ailments. The parts used in homoeopathy are the leaves and flowers and the remedy is of value in first aid for its antiseptic and anti-inflammatory activity. It is used in the treatment of boils, stings, cuts and wounds and to stem bleeding often in the form of an ointment which can be applied to broken skin. It is helpful when applied to skin tears following childbirth. It is used in the form of an antiseptic tincture as a mouth wash and gargle after tooth extraction, for mouth ulcers or a septic sore throat. When taken internally it prevents suppuration (pus formation) and may be used for persistent chronic ulcers and varicose ulcers, fever and jaundice. It is a useful remedy in the

treatment of children's ailments. The symptoms are made worse in damp, draughty conditions and cloudy weather and after eating. They improve with walking about and lying absolutely still.

Cantharis

Canth, Spanish Fly

This remedy is derived from the body and wings of a bright green, iridescent beetle which is found mainly in the southern parts of Spain and France. The beetle *Cantharis vesicatoria* secretes a substance called canthardin which has irritant properties and is also poisonous and is an ancient remedy to cure warts. It was also used as an aphrodisiac, reputedly by the notorious Marquis de Sade. The beetles are dried and ground to produce a powder which is then used in homoeopathy. It is an irritant, blistering agent acting externally on the part of the body to which it is applied and internally on the bladder, urinary tract and genital organs. Hence it is used to treat conditions in which there are stinging and burning pains. An accompanying symptom is often a great thirst but a reluctance to drink. It is used to treat cystitis with cutting hot pains on passing urine, urinary frequency with pain and other urinary infections. Also, certain inflammations of the digestive system in which there is abdominal distension and burning pains and diarrhoea. In general it is used as a remedy for conditions which worsen rapidly. It is a remedy for burns and scalds of the skin, including sunburn, insect stings and rashes with spots which contain pus. Some mental symptoms are eased by cantharis, including angry and irritable or violent behaviour, extreme anxiety and excessive sexual appetite. Symptoms are made worse with movement, touch and after drinking coffee or chilled water. They improve when gastrointestinal wind is eliminated and with warmth, at night time and with very light massage.

Carbo vegetabilis

Carbo veg, vegetable charcoal

This homoeopathic remedy is made from charcoal which itself is obtained from heating or partially burning wood without oxygen. The charcoal is hard and black or dark grey, and is a form of carbon which is present in all living things. Charcoal has been made for centuries and usually silver birch, beech or poplar trees are the source of wood which is used. The homoeopathic remedy is used to treat a person who is run down, weak or exhausted especially after a debilitating illness or operation. It is also used for postoperative shock when there is a clammy, cold, pale skin but the person feels a sensation of heat or burning inside. It is helpful as a remedy for ailments of poor circulation such as varicose veins. Again, the skin tends to be pale, clammy and chilly with a bluish colour and the extremities feel cold. The legs may be puffy and additional symptoms include hoarseness and laryngitis and lack of energy. This is a useful remedy for digestive problems and carbon is also used for this purpose in orthodox medicine. Symptoms are those of indigestion, heartburn and flatulence with a sour taste in the mouth. Morning headaches with accompanying symptoms of nausea and giddiness or fainting may be relieved by this preparation, particularly if the cause is a large, heavy meal the night before. People suitable for this remedy often complain of a lack of energy and may indeed be physically and mentally exhausted, with poor powers of concentration and lapses of memory. They usually have fixed attitudes with a lack of interest in news of the wider world. They do not like the night and are fearful of the supernatural. Symptoms are made worse by warm, moist weather, in the evening and night and with lying down. They are also exacerbated after eating meals of fatty foods, coffee and milk and drinks of wine. They improve with burping and with circulating cool, fresh air.

Chamomilla

Chamomile, Common Chamomile, Double Chamomile
A creeping and trailing plant which produces daisy-like flowers in summer and prefers dry, sandy soils. Chamomiles are native to Britain and others part of northern Europe and have been used in medicine since ancient times, being described by Hippocrates. When walked on, it gives off an aromatic perfume and was gathered and strewn on the floor in medieval dwellings to counter unpleasant odours. It is prized for its many medicinal uses, the flowers and leaves both being used for a number of different ailments. Herbalists use chamomile to treat skin conditions such as eczema, and for asthma and disturbed sleep. In homoeopathy, it is used for its soothing and sedative effect on all conditions producing restlessness, irritability and pains. It is a useful remedy for children's complaints such as teething where the child is fretful and cries if put down, colicky pains and disturbed sleep. Also, for toothache when one cheek is red and the other white and which is exacerbated by heat and relieved by cold. It is used to treat a blocked ear and earache, painful, heavy periods and breast soreness and inflammation associated with breast-feeding. People suitable for this remedy are very sensitive to pain and illness which causes sweating or fainting, especially in children and women. They are

irritable and fretful when ill. Symptoms are made worse if the person becomes angry or in cold winds and the open air. They improve if the person fasts for a time and if the weather is wet and warm. People who are suitable for chamomile are noisy sleepers in that they frequently cry out or talk while dreaming. If woken suddenly from sleep they are extremely irritable and they like to poke their feet out from the bed covers to keep them cool.

Cinchona officinalis

China, Peruvian Bark, Jesuits Bark

This homoeopathic remedy, known commonly as china, is obtained from the dried bark of the Cinchona tree and contains quinine. The attractive evergreen Cinchona, with its red bark, is a native of the hot tropical forests of South America, but it is also cultivated in India, Sri Lanka and south-east Asia. A preparation of powdered bark was used to treat a feverish illness suffered by the Countess of Cinchon, wife of the Viceroy of Peru in 1638. After her recovery she publicized the remedy and the tree was thus called Cinchona. The value of the bark as a cure for malaria had long been known and used by Jesuit priests. This was the first homoeopathic substance tested and proved by Hahnemann on himself.

In modern homoeopathy it is used mainly as a remedy for nervous and physical exhaustion resulting from chronic debilitating illnesses. It is used for weakness due to dehydration, sweating, chills and fever, and headaches that are relieved if firm pressure is applied. The person wants drinks during periods of chills and shivering, rather than when feverish and hot. He or she usually has a washed out, unhealthy complexion with very sensitive skin. China is also used as a remedy for neuralgia, muscles that twitch due to extreme fatigue, bleeding including nosebleeds and tinnitus or noises in the ears. It has a helpful effect on the digestion and is used to treat gastrointestinal wind, gall bladder disorders and digestive upset. Some mental symptoms are helped by this remedy including irritability and tetchy behaviour which is out of character, apathy and loss of concentration and sleeplessness.

People who are suitable for this remedy tend to be artistic, imaginative and highly strung. They find it easier to empathize with the natural world rather than with the people around them. They are intense and dislike trivial conversation and fatty foods such as butter, but have a liking for alcoholic drinks. Their nature makes them prone to irritability and depression and they tend to draw up grand schemes at night which are later abandoned. Symptoms are made better by warmth and plenty of sleep and by the application of steady continuous pressure to a painful area. They are made worse by cold, draughty weather, particularly in the autumn, and in the evening and night.

Citrullus colocynthus

Colocynthis; Bitter Cucumber, Bitter Apple

The plant *Citrillus colocynthis* is a native of Turkey, and is also found in parts of Asia and Africa flourishing in dry, arid conditions. It produces yellow flowers and then yellow/orange, smooth fruits, about the size of a large apple, which contain many seeds embedded in a whitish pulp. The homoeopathic remedy colocynthis is obtained from the dried fruits from which the seeds have been removed. This is then ground down to produce a powder. The fruit itself is poisonous, having a violent irritant effect on the digestive tract causing severe, cramp-like pains, inflammation and bleeding. This is caused by the presence of a substance called colocynthin. According to tradition, Elisha, the Old Testament prophet, is said to have performed a miraculous transformation of the fruit during the famine in Gilgal, making it fit for the people to eat. In homoeopathy, colocynthis is used to treat colicky abdominal pains which may be accompanied by sickness and diarrhoea (including colic in young babies). Also, for neuralgia, especially of the face, sciatica, ovarian or kidney pain due to nerves, rheumatic disorders and headache.

People who are helped by colocynthis are often reserved with a tendency to bottle-up anger. They have strong opinions about what is right and wrong and may become quite agitated if someone else has a contrary viewpoint. Physical symptoms of colicky pains or neuralgia and upset stomach may follow on from becoming upset or angry. The symptoms are made worse when the person becomes irritated or angry and in cold, damp weather conditions. Also, eating meals and drinking exacerbate the symptoms. They are relieved by warmth and pressure on the painful part and by drinking coffee. Abdominal flatulence also relieves the symptoms.

Cuprum metallicum

Cuprum met; copper

Copper ore, which is found in rocks in many parts of the world, has been mined and used for many centuries in the manufacture of weapons, utensils and jewellery etc. In earlier times, physicians made an ointment from the ground metal and this was applied to raw wounds to aid healing. Copper is poisonous in large doses, affecting the nervous system and causing convulsions, paralysis and possibly death due to its effects upon respiratory muscles. Toxic effects were recognized in those who worked with the metal and had developed wasting, due to poor absorption of food, coughs and respiratory symptoms and colicky pains. The ruddy, gold-coloured metal is ground to produce a fine red powder which is used in homoeopathy to treat cramping, colicky pains in the abdomen, and muscular spasms in the calves of the legs, feet and ankles. It is also used as a remedy for epilepsy and problems of breathing and respiration such as asthma, croup and whooping cough, in which there are spasms. The person may turn blue due to the effort of breathing.

The symptoms are made worse by touch, hot, sunny weather and for keeping emotions bottled up. They improve with sweating and for drinking cold fluids. People who benefit from this remedy have mood swings which alternate from stubbornness to passivity, weepiness and depression. They tend to be serious people who judge themselves severely and keep their emotions very much suppressed. As babies or toddlers, they may be breath-holders who turn blue with anger or as a result of a tantrum. As children, some are destructive and others are loners who dislike the company of others.

Daphne mezereum

Daphne, Spurge Laurel, Wild Pepper, Spurge Olive, Flowering Spurge, Dwarf Bay

This poisonous plant is native to upland areas of Europe and is cultivated in the United Kingdom. It produces cheerful bright-red flowers and dark green leaves and the bark is the part used in homoeopathy. It is used to treat skin conditions characterized by blistering especially erysipelas (an infection of the skin), shingles and varicose ulcers. Also, for any condition in which there is a persistent, dry cough, tightness around the chest and a mucus discharge from the nose. There may be burning pains which are worse at night.

Drosera rotundifolia

Drosera, Sundew, Youthwort, Red Rot, Moor Grass
This small, carnivorous (insect-eating) plant is found widely throughout Europe and in Britain, where it grows in the poor, acidic soils of bogs, damp uplands, moorlands and woodlands. It is a small plant growing close to the ground, and needs to trap insects for extra nutrients as the soil in which it grows is so poor. It is remarkable for its leaves which are covered with long red hairs each with a small, fluid-containing gland at the top.

When the sun shines on the leaves it resembles dew and hence the name, sundew. An insect landing on the leaf is trapped because the leaf curls over and inwards, and the sticky fluid secreted by the hairs holds the insect fast. The secretion contains enzymes which digest the body and the nutrients are absorbed by the plant. The small, white flowers of sundew are fully open in the early morning but close up when the sun is shining strongly.

In medieval times, the plant was used to treat tuberculosis and the plague, and it was employed as a remedy for skin disorders in early Asian medicine. It was noticed that sheep who inadvertently cropped sundew developed a paroxysmal type of cough like whooping cough. It was investigated and proved as a remedy for this illness in homoeopathy, and the whole plant is used to prepare the medicine. Any condition in which there is a violent, dry, persistent barking cough of a spasmodic nature, as in whooping cough, benefits from the use of sundew which has a particular action on the upper respiratory tract. Accompanying symptoms are gagging, sickness, sweating and nosebleeds. It is also used to treat bronchitis, asthma, corns and warts, growing pains and pains in the bones.

People who benefit from this remedy are restless and fearful of being alone when they are ill, and they tend to be stubborn and lacking in concentration. They are suspicious and may feel that others are talking about them or concealing bad news. They are sensitive to the supernatural and are afraid of ghosts. The symptoms are worse for being too warm in bed, after midnight, with crying, lying down, laughing, singing and talking. Also, for meals of cold food and drinks. Symptoms improve out in the fresh air, with walking or gentle exercise, sitting propped up in bed, with pressure applied to the painful part and in quiet surroundings.

Euphrasia officinalis

Euphrasia, Eyebright

Eyebright is an attractive wild flower which is variable in size and grows widely throughout Europe, including Britain and in North America. It has been known since medieval times as a remedy for inflammation of the eyes and this remains its main use in homoeopathy. The plant flourishes on well-drained, chalky soils and may be between two and eight inches in height depending upon conditions. It is partly parasitic, deriving some nourishment from the roots of grass and produces pretty white, purple-veined flowers with yellow centres. The whole plant and flowers are used in homoeopathy and the remedy is used to treat eye disorders characterized by redness, inflammation, watering, burning, stinging or itching. These include conjunctivitis, blepharitis (inflammation of eyelids), injuries to the eye and dry eyes. It is also used as a remedy for allergic conditions such as hay fever, in which the eyes are very much affected, and colds producing eye symptoms. It is a remedy for the early stages of measles, headaches, some menstrual problems and inflammation of the prostate gland in men. Symptoms are worse in the evening, in windy and warm weather and for being inside. They improve in subdued light, with drinking a cup of coffee and with cold applications.

Ferrum phosphoricum

Ferrum phos; Ferric Phosphate of iron, iron phosphate
Ferrum is one of the Schussler tissue salts and the iron phosphate powder is obtained by chemical reaction between sodium phosphate, sodium acetate and iron sulphate. Iron is a very important substance in the body, being found in the haemoglobin pigment of red blood cells, which transports oxygen to all the tissues and organs.

The homoeopathic remedy is used to treat the early stages of infections, inflammations and feverish conditions, before any other particular symptoms occur. It is used to treat colds and coughs in which there may be a slowly developing fever, headache, nosebleeds, bronchitis, hoarseness and loss of the voice, earache and rheumatic pains. Digestive symptoms such as sour indigestion, inflammation of the stomach (gastritis) and vomiting and some disorders of menstruation are helped by this remedy. It is also used to treat the early symptoms of dysentery. The person tends to be pale but is prone to flushing, and feels cold in the early afternoon. There may be a rapid weak pulse. Symptoms are worse at night and in the early morning between 4 a.m. and 6 a.m. Also, they are worse for heat and hot sun, movement and jarring of the body, pressure and touch and resting on the right side and suppressing sweating by the use of deodorants etc. Symptoms improve for cold applications and with gentle movements. People who are suitable for ferrum tend to be thin and pale but may be liable to flush easily. They are intelligent and quick to absorb new concepts, having plenty of original ideas of their own. They may be prone to digestive and respiratory complaints, stomach upsets and coughs and colds.

Gelsemium sempervirens

Gelsemium, Yellow Jasmine, False Jasmine, Carolina Jasmine, Wild Woodbine

This attractive climbing plant is a native of the southern United States and parts of Mexico. It has a woody stem which twists around any available tree trunk, and grows on stream banks and on the sea coast. It produces attractive, large, bell-shaped, perfumed yellow flowers in the early spring, which belie the poisonous nature of the plant. It has an underground stem or rhizome from which arise a tangle of yellow roots that have an aromatic smell. The root is the part used in homoeopathy and, if eaten in significant amounts, it affects the central nervous system causing paralysis and possible death through failure of the nerves and muscles of the respiratory system.

In homoeopathy, this remedy is used to treat both physical and mental symptoms. The physical ailments treated mainly involve the nervous and respiratory systems. These include headaches which are worsened with bright light and movement, multiple sclerosis, eye pain, especially on the right side, sore throat and influenza-like symptoms, earache and feverish muscular pains. Accompanying symptoms include chills and shivering, flushed face and malaise. It is used to treat some menstrual problems including pain. Mental symptoms which are helped by gelsemium include fears and phobias with symptoms of fatigue, weakness, trembling and apprehension. These fears may arise before an examination, interview or public performance (stage fright). Excitement or fear that causes the heart to skip a beat and extreme anxiety causing sleeplessness are helped by gelsemium. Symptoms are made worse in the sun and in warm, moist, humid weather or damp and fog. They are also worse with smoking and for excitement, anticipation, stress or bad news. Symptoms improve with movement in the fresh air and after sweating and drinking alcohol or a stimulant drink. They improve after urinating—a large quantity of pale urine is usually passed. People suitable for gelsemium tend to be well-built with a blue-tinged skin and often complain of feeling weak and tired. They are beset by fears and may be cowardly, and too fearful to lead or enjoy a normal active life.

Graphites

Graphite; Black pencil lead, Plumbago

Graphite is a form of carbon which is the basis of all life. It is found in older igneous or metamorphic rocks, such as granite and marble and is mined for its industrial uses in batteries, motors, pencil leads, cleaning and lubricating fluids. It was investigated and proved by Hahnemann after he learned that it was being used by some factory workers to heal cold sores. The powder used in homoeopathy is ground graphite and it is mainly used for skin disorders which may be caused by metabolic imbalances and stomach ulcers. It is a remedy for eczema, psoriasis, acne, rough, dry skin conditions with pustules or blisters, scarring and thickened cracked nails and cold sores. Also, for stomach ulcers due to a thinning or weakness in the lining of the stomach wall, problems caused by excessive catarrh, loss of hair and cramping pains or numbing of the feet and hands. In women it is used to treat some menstrual problems. The symptoms are worse in draughty, cold and damp conditions and for eating sweet meals or sea foods. Also, the use of steroids for skin complaints and, in women, during menstruation. Symptoms are often worse on the left side. They improve with warmth as long as the air is fresh and it is not stuffy, when it is dark and for eating and sleep. People suitable for graphites are usually well-built and may be overweight, often having dark hair. They like to eat well but lack physical fitness and sweat or flush with slight exertion. They are prone to dry, flaky skin conditions which may affect the scalp. Graphite people are usually lethargic and may be irritable, lacking in concentration for intellectual activities. They are prone to mood swings and subject to bouts of weeping, especially when listening to music. A graphite person is inclined to feel that he or she is unlucky and is inclined to self-pity, often feeling fearful and timid.

Guaiacum offinale

Guaiac, Resin of Lignum vitae

This attractive evergreen tree is a native of the West Indies and the northern coastal regions of South America. The tree grows to a height of 40–60 feet (12–18 metres) and produces striking, deep-blue flowers. The part used in homoeopathy is a resin obtained from the wood. The wood is unusual in being very dense which means that it sinks in water, and this property caused much interest when it was first discovered in the Middle Ages. The resin is obtained by firing the cut log, and the melted resin then flows out of a hole made in the wood and is collected. This is allowed to cool and harden and it is usually exported in large blocks which split readily into glassy fragments. The remedy is used to treat inflammation of the pharynx (pharyngitis) and tonsillitis being very helpful in relieving painful soreness of the throat. It is particularly indicated where there is foul-smelling sputum and sweating. It is also a remedy for gout and rheumatic conditions with severe and stabbing joint pains. The symptoms are made worse by extremes of heat and cold and damp weather and also with movement. They may be relieved by rest and keeping warm.

Hamamelis virginiana

Hamamelis, Witch Hazel, Spotted Alder, Snapping Hazelnut, Winterbloom

This plant is a native of the eastern United States and Canada but it is also grown in Europe. It is a shrub with grey/green leaves and yellow flowers which appear in the autumn. The part used in homoeopathy is the bark of stems and twigs and the outer part of the fresh root. This has the effect of causing body tissues, especially blood vessels, to contract and it is used to arrest bleeding. Its curative properties were known to the native North American Indians and it was first investigated and proved in homoeopathy by Dr Hering. Its main effect is on the blood circulation of the veins, particularly when the walls of the vessels are inflamed and weakened, and bleeding does not stop easily. It is used as a remedy for haemorrhoids (piles) with bleeding, varicose veins and ulcers, phlebitis (inflamed veins), nosebleeds, heavy periods, internal bleeding and pain associated with bruising or bleeding. Some headaches are helped by hamamelis and, also, mental symptoms of depression, irritability and impatience. The symptoms are made worse by warmth and moisture and with physical activity. They improve out in the fresh air and for concentrating on a particular task or event and for conversation, thinking and reading.

Hepar sulphuris calcareum

Hepar sulph; sulphide of calcium

This remedy is impure calcium sulphide, which is obtained by heating crushed and powdered oyster shells with flowers of sulphur. This is an old remedy which was, at one time, applied externally to treat swellings caused by tuberculosis, gout, rheumatism and thyroid disorders (including goitre) and also itching skin. It was investigated and proved by Hahnemann as a remedy for the toxic effects of mercury which was widely used by contemporary physicians. It is now used to treat infections and any condition where there is a discharge of foul-smelling pus. It is used to treat skin conditions where the skin is highly sensitive to touch, such as boils and acne and also, tonsillitis, sinusitis, earache, sore throat, hoarseness and laryngitis, mouth ulcers and cold sores. A wheezing, croup-type of cough, chesty cough which may develop into a cold or influenza is helped by hepar sulphuris. This remedy helps those who, when ill, tend to produce bodily secretions which have an unpleasant sour smell. During illness, those who benefit from this remedy are irritable, difficult to please and easily offended. They are difficult patients who make unreasonable demands and hate noise or disturbance, being touched or cold air. Symptoms are worse for cold and for getting chilled when undressing during Winter and for touch. They improve with warmth and warm applications, for covering the head and for eating a meal. People suitable for hepar tend to be overweight, lethargic with pale skin and often depressed. They feel that life has dealt with them harshly and feel the symptoms of illness and pain acutely. They may appear to be calm but tend to be anxious and restless.

Hypericum perfoliatum

Hypericum, St John's Wort

A perennial herbaceous plant which is a native of Britain, Europe and Asia, but is cultivated throughout the world. It grows between 1 and 3 feet (0.3–1 metre) in height producing elongated, oval, dark green leaves that appear to be covered in minute spots or holes (hence perfoliatum or perforate). In fact, these are minute oil-secreting glands that secrete a bright red solution. The large, bright yellow flowers appear in June, July and August and have small black dots around the edges of the petals. The crushed flowers produce a blood-coloured juice which was used, in early times, to treat raw wounds. It was also believed that the plant could be hung up to ward off evil spirits; (the name *Hypericum* being derived from the Greek meaning 'over an apparition'). There are two traditions associated with the common name, St John's Wort. One links the plant with 29th August, believed to be the anniversary of the execution of St John the Baptist. The other is that the plant is named after an ancient order of knights going back to the time of the Crusades, the Knights of St John of Jerusalem.

The whole fresh green plant and flowers are used in homoeopathy to produce the mother tincture. It is mainly used to treat damage to nerves and nerve pain following accidental injury. Typically, there are shooting, stabbing pains which radiate upwards and it is indicated especially where there are many nerve endings concentrated in a particular part of the body, e.g. the fingers and toes. It is very effective in pains associated with the spinal nerves and spinal cord, concussion, head or eye injuries. It is also a remedy for wounds and lacerations producing stabbing pains indicating nerve damage, and accidental crushing injuries. It is useful for bites, stings, splinters and puncture wounds, toothache and pain following dental extractions. In addition, it is a treatment for asthma and some digestive complaints of indigestion, sickness and diarrhoea. It is sometimes helpful in the treatment of haemorrhoids and some menstrual problems with accompanying headache. The symptoms are made worse by cold, damp or foggy weather, before a storm and through getting chilled when undressing. Also for touch and for a close, stuffy atmosphere. Symptoms improve when the person remains still and tilts the head backwards.

Ignatia amara

Ignatia; St Ignatius' Bean

Ignatia amara is a large tree which is native to the Philippine Islands, China and the East Indies. The tree has many branches and twining stems and produces stalked white flowers. Later, seed pods are produced, each containing ten to twenty large, oval seeds, that are about one inch long and are embedded in pulp. The seeds are highly poisonous and contain strychnine which affects the central nervous system. Similar active constituents and properties are found in nux vomica. The tree is named after the founder of the Jesuits, Ignatius Loyola (1491–1556), and Spanish priests belonging to this order brought the seeds to Europe during the 1600s.

The homoeopathic remedy is made from the powdered seeds and is used especially for emotional symptoms. It is used for grief, bereavement, shock and loss, particularly when a person is having difficulty coming to terms with his or her feelings and is inclined to suppress the natural responses. Accompanying symptoms include sleeplessness, anger and hysteria. Similar emotional and psychological problems are helped by this remedy, including anxiety and fear, especially a fear of appearing too forward to others, a tendency to burst into fits of crying, self-doubt, pity and blame and depression. Nervous tension headaches and digestive upsets, feverish symptoms, chills and pains in the abdomen may be helped by ignatia. Some problems associated with menstruation, especially sharp pains or absence of periods are relieved by this remedy as are conditions with changeable symptoms. These are worse in cold weather or conditions, with emotional trauma, being touched, for smoking and drinking coffee. They improve with warmth, moving about, eating, lying on the side or the area which is painful and after passing urine.

The person for whom ignatia is suitable is usually female with a tendency towards harsh, self-criticism and blame; she is usually a creative, artistic person, highly sensitive but with a tendency to suppress the emotions. She is perceptive and intelligent but inclined to be hysterical and subject to erratic swings of mood. Typically, the person expects a high standard in those she loves. The person enjoys dairy products, bread and sour foods but sweets, alcoholic drinks and fruit upset her system. She is afraid of crowds, tends to be claustrophobic, and fears being burgled. Also, she is afraid of being hurt emotionally, and is very sensitive to pain. The person is usually dark-haired and of slim build with a worried expression and prone to sighing, yawning and excessive blinking.

Ipecacuanha

Ipecac; Cephaelis ipecacuanha, Psychotria ipecacuanha, The Ipecac Plant

This plant is a native of South America, particularly Brazil, Bolivia and New Grenada. The plant contains the alkaloids, Emetine and cephaeline. Different varieties contain differing proportions of these alkaloids. The root is the part used in homoeopathy and the preparations may be in a number of different forms. It is used to treat conditions where the main symptoms are nausea and vomiting which are intractable and persistent, e.g. motion sickness and morning sickness. It is also used as a remedy for bronchitis, breathlessness due to the presence of fluid in the lung, whooping cough and heart failure. The symptoms are made worse by cold weather and lying down, and after a meal of pork or veal. They improve in the fresh open air and while resting with the eyes shut.

Kalium bichromicum

Kali bich; Potassium dichromate, potassium bichromate

This substance has several uses in industry (e.g in the preparations of dyes and in batteries) as well as its medicinal purposes. The crystals of potassium dichromate are bright orange and are prepared from a chemical reaction involving the addition of a solution of potassium chromate to an acid. It is used for discharges of mucus and disorders of the mucous membranes, particularly involving the vagina and genital and urinary tracts, throat, nose and stomach. The remedy is useful for catarrhal colds and sinusitis, feelings of fullness and pressure, headache, migraine and glue ear. Also, for joint and rheumatic disorders with pains that may move about or even disappear. People who benefit from this remedy are highly sensitive to cold and chills when ill, but also experience a worsening of symptoms in hot, sunny conditions. They tend to be people who adhere very closely to a regular routine and may be somewhat rigid and inflexible. They like everything to be done properly down to the smallest detail and are law-abiding, moral and conformist. Symptoms are worse during the summer and also in wet and chilly conditions. They are at their height in the early hours of the morning between 3 a.m. and 5 a.m. and also on first waking up. Drinking alcohol and becoming chilled while taking off clothes exacerbates the symptoms. They improve with moving around and after eating a meal. Also, symptoms improve with warmth and heat (but not hot sun) and after vomiting.

Kali iodatum

Kali iod; Kali hydriodicum, Potassium iodide

This is prepared by chemical reaction from potassium hydroxide and iodine and is an old remedy for syphilis. It is recommended that potassium iodide should be added to animal-feed concentrates and table salt to prevent deficiency in iodine. The homoeopathic remedy is used to relieve catarrh in those who are prone to chesty conditions. It is also used to treat swollen glands, sore throats, sinusitis, hay fever and influenza-type infections. It is used to treat male prostate gland disorders. The symptoms tend to improve with movement and from being out in the fresh air. They are made worse by heat and touch and are at their most severe between 2 a.m. and 5 a.m. People who suit this remedy tend to be dogmatic, knowing exactly what they think about a particular subject. They may be irritable or bad-tempered and not easy to get along with. They have a preference for cool rather than warm or hot weather.

Kali phosphoricum

Kali phos; Potassium Phosphate, phosphate of Potash
This remedy is one of the Schussler tissue salts and it is obtained from a chemical reaction between dilute phosphoric acid and solution of potassium carbonate. Potassium carbonate is derived from potash, the white powder which is left when wood is burnt completely. Potassium is an essential element in the body, vital for the healthy functioning of nerve tissue.

This remedy is used to treat mental and physical exhaustion and depression, particularly in young people in whom it may have been caused by too much work or study. Accompanying symptoms include jumping at noise or interruption and a desire to be alone. Also, there may be a pus-containing discharge from the bladder, vagina, bowels or lungs and extreme muscular fatigue. They may suffer from gnawing hunger pains, anxiety, insomnia and tremor with a tendency to perspire on the face when excited or after a meal.

People who are suitable for treatment with this remedy are usually extrovert, hold clearly-formed ideas and are easily exhausted. They become distressed by bad news, including that which does not affect them directly, such as a disaster in another country. They tend to crave sweet foods and dislike bread. Symptoms are made worse by any anxiety, in cold, dry weather, in winter and on drinking cold fluids. Also, they are exacerbated by noise, conversation, touch and physical activity. Symptoms improve with heat, gentle exercise, in cloudy conditions and after eating.

Lachesis trigonocephalus

Lachesis, venom of the Bushmaster or Surukuku snake
This South African snake produces a deadly venom which may prove instantly fatal due to its effects upon the heart. The venom causes the blood to thin and flow more freely, hence increasing the likelihood of haemorrhage. Even a slight bite bleeds copiously with a risk of blood poisoning or septicaemia. The snake is a ferocious hunter and its African name, *Surukuku*, describes the sound it makes while in pursuit of prey.

The properties of the venom were investigated by the eminent American homoeopathic doctor, Constantine Hering during the 1800s, who tested and proved the remedy on himself. It is effective in treating a variety of disorders, particularly those relating to the blood circulation and where there is a risk of blood poisoning or septicaemia. It is used to treat varicose veins and problems of the circulation indicated by a bluish tinge to the skin. The remedy is useful for those suffering from a weak heart or angina, palpitations and an irregular, fast or weak pulse. There may be symptoms of chest pain and breathing difficulty. It is of great benefit in treating uterine problems, particularly premenstrual congestion and pain that is relieved once the period starts. Also, this is an excellent remedy for menopausal symptoms, especially hot flushes, and for infections of the bladder and rectum. It is used to treat conditions and infections where symptoms are mainly on the left side, such as headache or stroke when the left side is involved. Also, as a treatment for sore throats and throat infections, tonsillitis, lung abscess, boils, ulcers, wounds which only heal slowly, vomiting due to appendicitis and digestive disorders, fevers with chills and shivering, nosebleeds and bleeding piles.

It is used to treat severe symptoms of measles and serious infections including scarlet fever and smallpox. Symptoms are made worse for touch and after sleep and by tight clothing. They are worse for hot drinks and baths, exposure to hot sun or direct heat in any form. For women, symptoms are worse during the menopause. They improve for being out in the fresh air and drinking cold drinks and for release of normal bodily discharges. Lachesis people tend to be intelligent, creative, intense and ambitious. They have strong views about politics and world affairs and may be impatient of the views of others. They may be somewhat self-centred, possessive and jealous which can cause problems in close relationships with others. They dislike being tied down and so may be reluctant to commit themselves to a relationship.

Lachesis people have a liking for sour pickled foods, bread, rice and oysters and alcoholic drinks. They like coffee, but hot drinks and wheat-based foods tend to upset them. They have a fear of water, people they do not know, being burgled and of dying or being suffocated. Physically, they may be overweight and are sometimes red-haired and freckled. Alternatively, they may be thin and dark-haired, pale and with a lot of energy. Children tend to be somewhat jealous of others and possessive of their friends, which can lead to naughty, trying behaviour.

Ledum palustre

Ledum; Marsh Tea, Wild Rosemary

Wild rosemary is an evergreen shrub which grows in the bogs and cold upland conditions of the northern United

States, Canada and Scandinavia, Ireland and parts of Asia. The bush produces elongated, dark green leaves about one or two inches long, which are smooth and shiny on the upper surface but underneath are covered with brown woolly hairs. (Ledum is derived from the Greek word *ledos*, meaning woolly robe). The leaves contain a volatile, aromatic oil, like camphor, and the plant has been used for centuries by Scandinavian people to repel insects, moths and mice. The plant produces attractive white flowers and is valued for its antiseptic properties. The fresh parts of the plant are gathered, dried and ground to make a powder used in homoeopathy and it is a valuable first aid remedy. It is taken internally for animal bites, insect stings, lacerations and wounds in which there is bruising and sharp stabbing pains. There is usually inflammation, redness, swelling and throbbing with feverish symptoms of chills and shivering. It is also used as a remedy for gout in the big toe, rheumatic pains in the feet which radiate upwards, hot, painful, stiff joints and tendons but with cold skin. People who benefit from this remedy tend to get hot and sweaty at night when ill, and usually throw off the bed coverings. They often have itchy skin on the feet and ankles and have a tendency to sprain their ankles. When ill, they are irritable and hard to please or may be withdrawn, and do not want the company of others. The symptoms are made worse by warmth or heat, touch and at night. They improve with cold applications to the painful part and for cool conditions.

Lycopodium clavatum

Lycopodium; Club Moss, Wolf's Claw, Vegetable Sulphur, Stagshorn Moss, Running Pine

This plant is found throughout the northern hemisphere,

in high moorlands, forests and mountains. The plant produces spore cases on the end of upright forked stalks which contain the spores. These produce yellow dust or powder which is resistant to water and was once used as a coating on pills and tablets to keep them separate from one another. The powder was also used as a constituent of fireworks. It has been used medicinally for many centuries, as a remedy for digestive disorders and kidney stones in Arabian countries and in the treatment of gout. The powder and spores are collected by shaking the fresh, flowering stalks of the plant and its main use in homoeopathy is for digestive and kidney disorders. It is used to treat indigestion, heartburn, the effects of eating a large meal late at night, sickness, nausea, wind, bloatedness and constipation. Also, in men, for kidney stones, with the production of a red-coloured urine containing a sand-like sediment and enlarged prostate gland. It is used in the treatment of some problems of male impotence and bleeding haemorrhoids or piles. Symptoms that occur on the right side are helped by lycopodium, and the patient additionally tends to crave sweet, comfort foods. Nettlerash, psoriasis affecting the hands, fatigue due to illness and ME (Myalgic encephalomyelitis), some types of headache, cough and sore throat are relieved by this remedy. It is used to relieve emotional states of anxiety, fear and apprehension caused by chronic insecurity, or relating to forthcoming events such as taking an examination or appearing in public (stage fright). Also, night terrors, sleeplessness, shouting or talking in the sleep and being frightened on first waking up can all benefit from this treatment.

The symptoms are worse between 4 p.m. and 8 p.m. and in warm, stuffy rooms and with wearing clothes which are too tight. They are also worse in the early morning between 4 a.m. and 8 a.m., for eating too much and during the spring. They improve outside in cool fresh air, after a hot meal or drink and with loosening tight clothing, with light exercise and at night. People suitable for lycopodium tend to be serious, hard-working and intelligent, often in professional positions. They seem to be self-possessed and confident but are, in reality, rather insecure with a low self-opinion. They are impatient of what they perceive as being weakness and are not tolerant or sympathetic of illness. Lycopodium people are sociable but may keep their distance and not get involved; they may be sexually promiscuous. They have a great liking for sweet foods of all kinds and enjoy hot meals and drinks. They are easily filled but may carry on eating regardless of this and usually complain of symptoms on the right side. Lycopodium people are afraid of being left on their own, of failure in life, of crowds, darkness and the supernatural and tend to be claustrophobic. They are often tall, thin and pale with receding hair or hair that turns grey early in life. They may be bald, with a forehead lined with worry lines and a serious appearance. They tend to have weak muscles and are easily tired after physical exercise. They may have a tendency to unconsciously twitch the muscles of the face and to flare the nostrils.

Mercurius solubilis

Merc sol; Quicksilver

The mineral cinnabar, which is found in volcanic crystalline rocks, is an important ore of mercury and is extracted for a variety of uses, including dental fillings and in thermometers. Mercury is toxic in large doses, and an affected person produces copious quantities of saliva and suffers repeated bouts of vomiting. Mercury has been used since ancient times and was once given as a remedy for syphilis. A powder of precipitate of mercury is obtained from dissolving liquid mercury in a dilute solution of nitric acid and this is the source of the remedy used in homoeopathy. It is used as a remedy for conditions which produce copious bodily secretions that often smell unpleasant, with accompanying symptoms of heat or burning and a great sensitivity to temperature. It is used as a remedy for fevers with profuse, unpleasant sweating, bad breath, inflammation of the gums, mouth ulcers, Candidiasis (thrush) of the mouth, infected painful teeth and gums and excessive production of saliva. Also, for a sore infected throat, tonsillitis, mumps, discharging infected ear and a congested severe headache and pains in the joints. It is good for eye complaints including severe conjunctivitis, allergic conditions with a running nose, skin complaints which produce pus-filled blisters, spots and ulcers, including varicose ulcers. The symptoms are made worse by extremes of heat and cold and also for wet and rapidly changing weather. They are worse at night and for sweating and being too hot in bed.

Symptoms improve for rest and in comfortable temperatures where the person is neither too hot nor too cold. People suitable for this remedy tend to be very insecure although they have an outwardly calm appearance. They are cautious and reserved with other people and consider what they are about to say before speaking so that conversation may seem laboured. These types do not like criticism of any kind and may suddenly become angry if someone disagrees with their point of view. They tend to be introverted but their innermost thoughts may be in turmoil. They tend to be hungry and enjoy bread and butter, milk and other cold drinks but dislike alcohol with the exception of beer. They usually do not eat meat, dislike coffee and salt and do not have a sweet tooth. People who benefit from this remedy often have fair hair with fine, unlined skin and an air of detachment. They are afraid of dying and of mental illness leading to insanity, and worry about the wellbeing of their family. They fear being burgled and are afraid or fearful during a thunderstorm.

Natrum muriaticum

Nat mur; table salt, sodium chloride

Salt has long been prized for its seasoning and preservative qualities, and Roman soldiers were once paid in salt, such was its value. (Salary comes from the Latin word *salarium*, which refers to this practice). Sodium and chlorine are essential chemicals in the body, being needed for many metabolic processes, particularly the functioning of nerve tissue. In fact, there is seldom a need to add salt to food as usually enough is present naturally in a healthy, well-balanced diet. (An exception is when people are working very hard physically in a hot climate and losing a lot of salt in sweat). However, people and many other mammals frequently have a great liking for salt. If the salt/water balance in the body is disturbed, a person soon becomes very ill and may even die. In ancient times, salt was usually obtained by boiling sea water, but natural evaporation around the shallow edges of salt lakes results in deposits of rock salt being formed. Rock salt is the usual source of table salt and also of the remedy used in homoeopathy. This remedy has an effect on the functioning of the kidneys and the salt/water balance of body fluids, and is used to treat both mental and physical symptoms. Emotional symptoms that benefit from this remedy include sensitivity and irritability, tearfulness and depression, suppressed grief and premenstrual tension. Physical ailments that respond to this remedy are often those in which there is a thin, watery discharge of mucus and in which symptoms are made worse by heat. Hence it is used in the treatment of colds with a runny nose or other catarrhal problems. Also, for some menstrual and vaginal problems, headaches and migraines, cold sores, Candidiasis (thrush) of the mouth, mouth ulcers, inflamed and infected gums and bad breath. Some skin disorders are helped by this remedy including verruca (a wart on the foot), warts, spots and boils and cracked, dry lips. It may be used in the treatment of fluid retention with puffiness around the face, eyelids and abdomen etc., urine retention, constipation, anal fissure, indigestion, anaemia and goitre. When ill, people who benefit from natrum muriaticum feel cold and shivery but their symptoms are made worse, or even brought on, by heat. Heat, whether from hot sun and fire or a warm, stuffy room exacerbate the symptoms which also are made worse in cold and thundery weather. They are worse on the coast from the sea breeze, and between 9 a.m. and 11 a.m. Too much physical activity and the sympathy of others exacerbate the symptoms. They improve in the fresh, open air and for cold applications or a cold bath or swim. Also, sleeping on a hard bed and sweating and fasting make the symptoms better. People suitable for this preparation are often women who are highly sensitive, serious-minded, intelligent and reliable. They have high ideals and feel things very deeply being easily hurt and stung by slights and criticism. They need the company of other people but, being so sensitive, can actually shun them for fear of being hurt. They are afraid of mental illness leading to loss of self-control and insanity and of dying. Also, they fear the dark, failure in work, crowds, being burgled and have a tendency to be claustrophobic. They worry about being late, are fearful during a thunderstorm and tend to become introverted and react badly to the criticism of others. They are highly sensitive to the influence of music which easily moves them to tears. Also they are usually of squat or solid build with dark or fairish hair. They are prone to reddened, watery eyes as though they have been crying, and a cracked lower lip. The face may appear puffy and shiny with an air of stoicism.

Nux vomica

Strychnos Nux vomica; Poison Nut, Quaker Buttons
The Strychnos Nux vomica tree is a native of India but also grows in Burma, Thailand, China and Australia. It produces small, greenish-white flowers and later, apple-sized fruits, containing small, flat, circular, pale seeds covered in fine hair. The seeds, bark and leaves are highly poisonous, containing strychnine, and have been used in medicine for many centuries. In medieval times, the seeds were used as a treatment for the plague. Strychnine has severe effects upon the nervous system but in minute amounts can help increase urination and aid digestion. The seeds are cleaned and dried and used to produce the homoeopathic remedy. Nux vomica is used in the treatment of a variety of digestive complaints including cramping, colicky abdominal pains, indigestion, nausea and vomiting, diarrhoea and constipation. Also, indigestion or stomach upset caused by overindulgence in alcohol or rich food and piles which cause painful contractions of the rectum. Sometimes, these complaints are brought on by a tendency to keep emotions,

particularly anger, suppressed and not allowing it to show or be expressed outwardly. Nux vomica is a remedy for irritability, headache and migraine, colds, coughs and influenza-like symptoms of fever, aching bones and muscles and chills and shivering. It is a useful remedy for women who experience heavy, painful periods which may cause fainting, morning sickness during pregnancy and pain in labour. It is also used to treat urinary frequency and cystitis.

The type of person who benefits from this remedy is frequently under stress and experiences a periodic flare-up of symptoms. The person may be prone to indigestion and heartburn, gastritis and stomach ulcer and piles. The person usually has a tendency to keep everything bottled up but has a passionate nature and is liable to outbursts of anger. Nux vomica people are very ambitious and competitive, demanding a high standard of themselves and others and intolerant of anything less than perfection. They enjoy challenges and using their wits to keep one step ahead. Often, they are to be found as managers, company directors, scientists, etc.—at the cutting edge of their particular occupation. They are ungracious and irritable when ill and cannot abide the criticism of others.

This type of person is afraid of being a failure at work and fears or dislikes crowded public places. He or she is afraid of dying. The person enjoys rich, fattening foods containing cholesterol and spicy meals, alcohol and coffee although these upset the digestive system. Symptoms are worse in cold, windy, dry weather and in winter and in the early morning between 3 a.m. and 4 a.m. They are aggravated by certain noises, music, bright lights and touch, eating (especially spicy meals) and for overwork of mental faculties. Nux vomica people usually tend to look serious, tense and are thin with a worried expression. They have sallow skin and tend to have dark shadows beneath the eyes.

Phosphorus

Phos; White Phosphorus

Phosphorus is an essential mineral in the body found in the genetical material (DNA), bones and teeth. White phosphorus is extremely flammable and poisonous and was once used in the manufacture of matches and fireworks. Due to the fact that it tends to catch fire spontaneously when exposed to air, it is stored under water. In the past it has been used to treat a number of disorders and infectious diseases such as measles. In homoeopathy, the remedy is used to treat nervous tension caused by stress and worry, with symptoms of sleeplessness, exhaustion and digestive upset. Often there are pains of a burning nature in the chest or abdomen. It is a remedy for vomiting and nausea, heartburn, acid indigestion, stomach ulcer and gastroenteritis. It is also used to treat bleeding, e.g. from minor wounds, the gums, nosebleeds, gastric and profuse menstrual bleeding.

Severe coughs which may be accompanied by retching, vomiting and production of a blood-tinged phlegm are treated with phosphorus, as well as some other severe respiratory complaints. These include pneumonia, bronchitis, asthma and laryngitis. Styes that tend to recur and poor circulation may be helped by phosphorus. Symptoms are worse in the evening and morning and before or during a thunderstorm. They are also made worse for too much physical activity, hot food and drink and lying on the left side. Symptoms improve in the fresh open air and with lying on the back or right side. They are better after sleep or when the person is touched or stroked. People who need phosphorus do not like to be alone when ill and improve for the sympathy and attention of others. They are warm, kind, affectionate people who are highly creative, imaginative and artistic. They enjoy the company of other people and need stimulation to give impetus to their ideas. Phosphorus people have an optimistic outlook, are full of enthusiasm but sometimes promise much and deliver little. They are very tactile and like to be touched or stroked and offered sympathy when unhappy or unwell. They enjoy a variety of different foods but tend to suffer from digestive upsets. Phosphorus people are usually tall, slim and may be dark or fair-haired, with an attractive, open appearance. They like to wear brightly coloured clothes and are usually popular with many friends. They have a fear of illness, especially cancer, and of dying and also of the dark and supernatural forces. They are apprehensive of water and fear being a failure in their work. Thunderstorms make them nervous.

Pulsatilla nigricans

Pulsatilla, Anemone pratensis, Meadow Anemone
This attractive plant closely resembles *Anemone pulsatilla*, the Pasque flower, which is used in herbal medicine, but has smaller flowers. Anemone pratensis is a native of Germany, Denmark and Scandinavia and has been used medicinally for hundreds of years. The plant produces beautiful deep purple flowers with orange centres and both leaves and flowers are covered with fine, silky hairs. The whole fresh plant is gathered and made into a pulp and liquid is extracted to make the remedy used in homoeopathy. It is used to treat a wide variety of disorders with both physical and mental

symptoms. It is a useful remedy for ailments, in which there is a greenish/yellowish discharge. Hence it is used for colds and coughs and sinusitis, with the production of profuse catarrh or phlegm. Also, eye infections with discharge such as styes and conjunctivitis. Digestive disorders are helped by pulsatilla, particularly indigestion, heartburn, nausea and sickness caused by eating too much fatty or rich food. The remedy is helpful for female disorders in which there are a variety of physical and emotional symptoms. These include premenstrual tension, menstrual problems, menopausal symptoms and cystitis, with accompanying symptoms of mood swings, depression and tearfulness. It is a remedy for headaches and migraine, swollen glands, inflammation and pain in the bones and joints as in rheumatic and arthritic disorders, nosebleeds, varicose veins, mumps, measles, toothache, acne, frequent urination and incontinence.

Symptoms are worse at night or when it is hot, and after eating heavy, rich food. Symptoms improve out in the cool fresh air and for gentle exercise such as walking. The person feels better after crying and being treated sympathetically by others. Pulsatilla people are usually women who have a mild, passive nature and are kind, gentle and loving. They are easily moved to tears by the plight of others and love animals and people alike. The person yields easily to the requests and demands of others and is a peacemaker who likes to avoid a scene. An outburst of anger is very much out of character and a pulsatilla person usually has many friends. The person likes rich and sweet foods, although these may upset the digestion, and dislikes spicy meals. Pulsatilla people may fear darkness, being left alone, dying and any illness leading to insanity. They are fearful of crowds, the supernatural and tend to be claustrophobic. Usually, they are fair and blue-eyed with clear, delicate skin which blushes readily. They are attractive and slightly overweight or plump.

Rhus toxicodendron

Rhus tox.; Rhus radicaris, American Poison Ivy, Poison Oak, Poison Vine.

This large bush or small tree is a native species of the United States and Canada. Its leaves are extremely irritant to the touch, causing an inflamed and painful rash, swelling and ulceration. Often the person experiences malaise, swollen glands, headache, feverishness and a lack of appetite. The plant produces white flowers with a green or yellow tinge in June, followed later by clusters of berries. The fresh leaves are gathered and pulped to make the remedy used in homoeopathy. It is used especially as a treatment for skin rashes and lesions with hot, burning sensations and also for inflammation of muscles and joints. Hence it is used to treat eczema, chilblains, cold sores, shingles, nappy rash and other conditions in which there is a dry, scaling or blistered skin. Also, for rheumatism, sciatica, lumbago, gout, synovitis (inflammation of the synovial membranes surrounding joints), osteoarthritis, ligament and tendon strains. Feverish symptoms due to viral infections such as high temperature, chills and shivering, swollen, watering eyes, aching joints, nausea and vomiting may be helped by Rhus. Some menstrual problems, including heavy bleeding and abdominal pains which are relieved by lying down, benefit from this remedy. People who are helped by this remedy tend to be depressed and miserable when ill, with a tendency to burst into tears and are highly susceptible to cold, damp weather.

Usually, they have a dry, irritating cough and thirst and are irritable, anxious and restless. The symptoms are made worse in stormy, wet, windy weather and at night, and when the person moves after a period of rest. Also for becoming chilled when undressing. Warm, dry conditions and gentle exercise improve and lessen the symptoms. People who benefit from this preparation may be initially shy in company but when they lose this are charming, entertaining and lively and make friends easily. They are usually conscientious and highly motivated and serious about their work to the extent of being a workaholic. Rhus people often have an inner restlessness and become depressed and moody when affected by illness. They may be prone to carry out small compulsive rituals in order to function.

Ruta graveolens

Ruta grav; Rue, Garden Rue, Herbygrass, Ave-grace, Herb-of-Grace, Bitter Herb

This hardy, evergreen plant is a native of southern Europe but has been cultivated in Britain for centuries, having been first brought here by the Romans. It thrives in poor soil in a dry and partially shaded situation, producing yellow-green flowers. The whole plant has a distinctive, pungent, unpleasant smell and was once used to repel insects, pestilence and infections. It has been used medicinally throughout history to treat ailments in both animals and people, and was used to guard against the plague. It was believed to be effective in guarding against witchcraft and Hippocrates recommended it as an antidote to poisoning. Rue was believed to have beneficial effects on sight and was used by the great artists such as Michelangelo to keep vision sharp. In the Catholic High Mass, brushes made from Rue were once used to sprinkle the holy water, hence Herb-of-Grace. Taken internally in large doses, Rue has toxic effects causing vomiting, a swollen tongue, fits and delirium.

The homoeopathic remedy is prepared from the sap of the green parts of the plant before the flowers open. It is indicated especially for bone and joint injuries and disorders, and those affecting tendons, ligaments and muscles where there is severe, deep, tearing pain. Hence it is used for synovitis (inflammation of the synovial membranes lining joints), rheumatism, sprains, strains, bruising, fractures and dislocations and also sciatica. Also, it is a useful remedy for eyestrain with tired, aching eyes, redness and inflammation and headache. Chest problems may be relieved by this preparation, particularly painful deep coughs, and some problems affecting the rectum such as prolapse. Pain and infection in the socket of a tooth after dental extraction may be helped by this remedy. A person who is ill tends to feel low, anxious, depressed and dissatisfied both with himself (or herself) and others. The symptoms are usually worse in cold, damp weather, for resting and lying down and for exercise out of doors. They improve with heat and gentle movement indoors.

Sepia officinalis

Sepia; ink of the cuttlefish
Cuttlefish ink has been used since ancient times, both for medicinal purposes and as a colour in artists' paint. The cuttlefish has the ability to change colour to blend in with its surroundings and squirts out the dark brown/ black ink when threatened by predators. Sepia was known to Roman physicians who used it as a cure for baldness. In homoeopathy it is mainly used as an excellent remedy for women experiencing menstrual and

menopausal problems. It was investigated and proved by Hahnemann in 1834. It is used to treat premenstrual tension, menstrual pain and heavy bleeding, infrequent or suppressed periods, menopausal symptoms such as hot flushes and postnatal depression. Physical and emotional symptoms caused by an imbalance of hormones are helped by sepia. Also, conditions in which there is extreme fatigue or exhaustion with muscular aches and pains. Digestive complaints, including nausea and sickness, abdominal pain and wind, caused by eating dairy products, and headaches with giddiness and nausea are relieved by sepia. Also, it is a remedy for incontinence, hot, sweaty feet and verruca (a wart on the foot). Disorders of the circulation, especially varicose veins and cold extremities benefit from sepia.

Symptoms are worse in cold weather and before a thunderstorm and in the late afternoon, evening and early in the morning. Also, before menstruation in women and if the person receives sympathy from others. The symptoms are better with heat and warmth, quick vigorous movements, having plenty to do and out in the fresh open air. People suitable for sepia are usually, but not exclusively, women. They tend to be tall, thin and with a yellowish complexion and are rather self-contained and indifferent to others. Sepia people may become easily cross, especially with family and close friends and harbour resentment. In company, they make a great effort to appear outgoing and love to dance. A woman may be either an externally hard, successful career person or someone who constantly feels unable to cope, especially with looking after the home and family. Sepia people have strongly held beliefs and cannot stand others taking a contrary opinion. When ill, they hate to be fussed over or have the sympathy of others. They like both sour and sweet foods and alcoholic drinks but are upset by milk products and fatty meals. They harbour deep insecurity and fear being left alone, illness resulting in madness and loss of their material possessions and wealth. One physical attribute is that they often have a brown mark in the shape of a saddle across the bridge of the nose.

Silicea terra

Silicea; silica

Silica is one of the main rock-forming minerals and is also found in living things, where its main function is to confer strength and resilience. In homoeopathy, it is used to treat disorders of the skin, nails and bones and recurring inflammations and infections, especially those which occur because the person is somewhat run-down or has an inadequate diet. Also, some disorders of the nervous system are relieved by silicea. The homoeopathic remedy used to be derived from ground flint or quartz but is now prepared by chemical reaction. The remedy is used for catarrhal infections such as colds, influenza, sinusitis and ear infections including glue ear. Also, for inflammations producing pus such as a boil, carbuncle, abscess, stye, whitlow (infection of the finger nail) and peritonsillar abscess. It is beneficial in helping the natural expulsion of a foreign body such as a splinter in the skin. It is a remedy for a headache beginning at the back of the head and radiating forwards over the right eye and for stress-related conditions of over-work and sleeplessness.

Symptoms are worse for cold, wet weather, especially when clothing is inadequate, draughts, swimming and bathing, becoming chilled after removing clothes and in the morning. They are better for warmth and heat, summer weather, warm clothing, particularly a hat or head covering, and not lying on the left side. People who are suitable for silicea tend to be thin with a fine build and pale skin. They often have thin, straight hair. They are prone to dry, cracked skin and nails and may suffer from skin infections. Silicea people are usually unassuming, and lacking in confidence and physical stamina. They are conscientious and hard-working to the point of working too hard once a task has been undertaken. However, they may hesitate to commit themselves through lack of confidence and fear of responsibility. Silicea people are tidy and obsessive about small details. They may feel 'put upon', but lack the courage to speak out, and may take this out on others who are not responsible for the situation. They fear failure and dislike exercise due to physical weakness, often feeling mentally and physically exhausted. They enjoy cold foods and drinks.

Sulphur

Sulphur, Flowers of sulphur, brimstone

Sulphur has a long history of use in medicine going back to very ancient times. Sulphur gives off sulphur dioxide when burnt which smells unpleasant ('rotten eggs' odour), but acts as a disinfectant. This was used in medieval times to limit the spread of infectious diseases. Sulphur is deposited around the edges of hot springs and geysers and where there is volcanic activity. Flowers of sulphur, which is a bright yellow powder, is obtained from the natural mineral deposit and is used to make the homoeopathic remedy. Sulphur is found naturally in all body tissues and, in both orthodox medicine and homoeopathy, is used to treat skin disorders. It is a useful remedy for dermatitis, eczema, psoriasis and a dry, flaky, itchy skin or scalp. Some digestive disorders benefit from sulphur especially a tendency for food to rise back up to the mouth and indigestion caused by drinking milk. Sulphur is helpful in the treatment of haemorrhoids, premenstrual and menopausal symptoms, eye inflammations such as conjunctivitis, pain in the lower part of the back, catarrhal colds and coughs, migraine headaches and feverish symptoms. Some mental symptoms are helped by this remedy particularly those brought about by stress or worry including depression, irritability, insomnia and lethargy. When ill, people who benefit from sulphur feel thirsty rather than hungry and are upset by unpleasant smells. The person soon becomes exhausted and usually sleeps poorly at night and is tired through the day. The symptoms are worse in cold, damp conditions, in the middle of the morning around 11 a.m. and in stuffy, hot, airless rooms. Also, for becoming too hot at night in bed and for wearing too many layers of clothes. Long periods of standing and sitting aggravate the symptoms and they are worse if the person drinks alcohol or has a wash. Symptoms improve in dry, clear, warm weather and for taking exercise. They are better if the person lies on the right side.

Sulphur people tend to look rather untidy and have dry, flaky skin and coarse, rough hair. They may be thin, round-shouldered and inclined to slouch or be overweight, round and red-faced. Sulphur people have lively, intelligent minds full of schemes and inventions, but are often useless on a practical level. They may be somewhat self-centred with a need to be praised, and fussy over small unimportant details. They enjoy intellectual discussion on subjects which they find interesting and may become quite heated although the anger soon subsides. Sulphur people are often warm and generous with their time and money. They enjoy a wide range of foods but are upset by milk and eggs. They have a fear of being a failure in their work, of heights and the supernatural.

Tarentula cubensis

Tarentula Cub; Cuban Tarantula

The bite of the Cuban Tarantula spider produces a delayed response in the victim. About 24 hours after a bite, the site becomes inflamed and red and a swelling, fever and abscess follow. The homoeopathic remedy, made from the poison of the spider is used to treat similar septic conditions such as an abscess, boil, carbuncle or whitlow (an infection of the finger nail) and genital itching. Also, it is a remedy for anthrax and shock and is of value as a last resort treatment in severe conditions. The infected areas are often tinged blue and there may be burning sensations of pain which are especially severe at night. It is of particular value in the treatment of recurring boils or carbuncles. The symptoms tend to improve with smoking and are made worse by physical activity and consuming cold drinks.

Thuja occidentalis

Thuja; Tree of Life, Yellow Cedar, Arbor Vitae, False White Cedar

This coniferous, evergreen tree is a native species of the northern United States and Canada and grows to a height of about 30 feet (9 metres). It has feathery green leaves with a strong, aromatic smell resembling that of camphor. The leaves and twigs were used by the Indian peoples to treat a variety of infections and disorders and the plant has long been used in herbal medicine. It is an important remedy in aromatherapy. The fresh green leaves and twigs are used to prepare the homoeopathic remedy, which is especially valuable in the treatment of warts and wart-like tumours on any part of the body. It is a useful remedy for shingles and also has an effect on the genital and urinary tracts. Hence it is used to treat inflammations and infections such as cystitis and urethritis and also pain on ovulation. It may be given as a remedy for infections of the mouth, teeth and gums, catarrh and for tension headaches.

People who benefit from thuja tend to sweat profusely and it helps to alleviate this symptom. They tend to suffer from insomnia and when they do manage to sleep, may talk or cry out. They are prone to severe left-sided frontal headaches which may be present on waking in the morning. Symptoms are worse at night, from being too hot in bed and after breakfast. Also, at 3 a.m. and 3 p.m. and in weather which is cold and wet. Symptoms are felt more severely on the left side. Symptoms improve for movement and stretching of the limbs, massage and after sweating. People suitable for thuja tend to be insecure and unsure about themselves. They try hard to please others but are very sensitive to criticism and soon become depressed. This may lead them to neglect their appearance. Thuja people are often thin and pale and tend to have greasy skin and perspire easily.

Urtica urens

Urtica; stinging nettle

One of the few plants that is familiar to all and which, for hundreds of years, has been valued for its medicinal and culinary uses. Nettles have always been used as a source of food both for people and animals, the young leaves being a nutritious vegetable with a high content of vitamin C. Nettles were thought to purify the blood and an ancient cure for rheumatism and muscular weakness was the practice of 'urtication', or lashing the body with stinging nettles. The hairs covering the leaves of the nettle release a volatile liquid when touched, which causes the familiar skin reaction of painful, white bumps to appear. The fresh, green parts of the plant are used to prepare the homoeopathic remedy which is used as a treatment for burning and stinging of the skin. Hence it is used to treat allergic reactions of the skin, urticaria or nettle rash, insect bites and stings and skin lesions due to burns and scalds. Also, for eczema, chicken pox, nerve inflammation and pain (neuritis and neuralgia), shingles, rheumatism, gout and cystitis in which there are burning, stinging pains. The person who benefits from this remedy is prone to inflamed, itching and irritated skin complaints and may be fretful, impatient and restless. Symptoms are made worse by touch and in cold, wet weather, snow and for contact with water. Allergic skin reactions may occur if the person eats shellfish such as prawns. The symptoms improve if the affected skin is rubbed and also if the person rests and lies down.